CIRCULAR OF INSTRUCTIONS

TO THE

COUNTY SURVEYORS

OF

NEBRASKA

ISSUED
MARCH 16, 1914
REPRINT 2014

ISBN: 978-0-9679041-5-3

Library of Congress Control Number: 2014931597

Preface to Reprint

The law of 1903 provided that the state surveyor should prepare and issue, under the direction of the Commissioner of Public Lands and Buildings, a circular of instructions to county surveyors. These instructions would be for their direction and guidance in the restoration and establishment of lines and preservation of corners in conformity with the laws, rules, and regulations of the United States, and the established rules of surveying; and for the concise and comprehensive preparation of field notes and maps of surveys. In compliance with the law, State Surveyor, Robert Harvey, prepared a pamphlet in late 1903 and had 500 copies printed under the title *"Circular of Instructions to County Surveyors"*. Copies were mailed to all Nebraska county surveyors and their deputies. In this circular, all subjects usually discussed in text books and manuals on surveying were avoided. Particular attention was given to how original corners were constructed and witnessed in the prairie country. Harvey discussed how numerous townships were subdivided into sections by what he designated the "Short Cut Method". He detailed the retracement of lines, the law for restoration of "Lost or Obliterated Corners", and the evidence by which corners and their witnesses, such as the "Trench and Pits" in the early surveys of the state, and later by the "Witness Pits". Harvey provided details on how to subdivide the fractional sections into their legal subdivisions, especially Section 6. He also addressed field books and official records.

This was the first appearance of a publication not only specific as to these subjects, but also on how to search for corners in the prairie country. Knowledge of this valuable publication quickly became widespread outside the borders of Nebraska. Requests for this circular came from surveyors and landowners, lawyers and judges, and universities, as well as, from the General Land Office in Washington, D. C. The original supply was quickly exhausted so printing another edition was imperative.

The new and expanded second edition contained over ten years of new information and was published in 1914 with 1,000 copies printed; of these, 106 were bound in leather for the use of the county surveyors and the remainder were printed in gray paper covers.

Before his death in 1923, Harvey had anticipated writing a third edition. Among the new topics he wanted to cover were several important court cases involving surveying, defining the center of a stream or river channel, and accretion issues.

One hundred years have passed since the second edition of *"Circular of Instructions to County Surveyors"* was published. The manner in which surveyors measure upon the ground has changed several times during the past century with new technology, but the importance of finding the correct monuments will never change.

Harvey said it best when he stated that it was the fault of many surveyors to treat corners as *lost* whose existence was not readily found on the surface or after a brief and careless search, when in fact every source of information that afforded a clue was not carefully examined. He also stated that the surveyor should make every effort to find the exact location of the missing corner or line, and that his aim should be to find where the corner or line was, and not where it ought to be.

It is my hope that the practices detailed by Harvey in his republished pamphlet will inspire surveyors to strive to a similar level of ethical standards in this modern world so as to avoid future problems resulting from careless or substandard work.

Care has been given to republish this publication exactly as it appeared, with only a few minor corrections in grammar.

Jerold F. Penry - 2014

[Begin Original Pamphlet – Next Page]

CIRCULAR OF INSTRUCTIONS

TO THE

COUNTY SURVEYORS

OF

NEBRASKA

ISSUED
MARCH 16, 1914

By
ROBERT HARVEY

State Surveyor and Draughtsman

BY AUTHORITY OF
FRED BECKMANN

Commissioner of Public Lands and Buildings and Custodian of Government Field Notes, Maps, Etc.

CHAFEE LIMESTONE MONUMENT

Erected October 1, 1869, to mark intersection of 25° W. long. from Washington, D. C., and 40° N. lat. for S. W. corner of Nebraska. Point determined from 97 Stellar observations. Monument stands 615½ feet south of the Kansas-Nebraska line on 25th meridian. Stone mutilated by curio seekers. Photographed May 11, 1910.

OFFICE OF

Commissioner of Public Lands and Buildings

DEPARTMENT OF SURVEYING

———————

OFFICERS:

FRED BECKMANN..Commissioner

G. E. EMERY...Deputy

ROBERT HARVEY.....................State Surveyor and Draughtsman

LINCOLN, NEBRASKA, March 16, 1914.

FRED BECKMANN,

Commissioner of Public Lands and Buildings.

SIR: I herewith submit for your approval this Second Edition of the Circular of Instructions to the County Surveyors of Nebraska.

In its preparation I have avoided all subjects which may be found in any of the text books on surveying, and confined the discussion mostly to such matters not usually found in print.

In the First Edition, published November 3, 1903, I called the particular attention of the surveyors to what I denominated the "short cut" method of subdividing townships by Government surveyors, which was the first appearance in print of a true explanation of the many irregularities in original surveys, especially of the long and short half miles of *East* and *West* lines of subdivisions and of "breaks" in many of the north and south lines, which was mainly due to "politics" making the Surveyor General's offices of the different states "Clearing Houses" for the payment of debts, for faithful political service, and not as heretofore attributed to the intoxication of the surveying force.

I also called attention to the discussion of "The Evidence of Trees, Trench and Pits," which is, so far as it relates to the "Trench and Pits," a discussion of an entirely new subject, which was not at that time found in any manual of surveying, or any Circular of Instructions issued by the General Land Office, or in any Pocket Manual or Text Book. In this edition the discussion has been extended to cover additional phases of this interesting subject, also additional suggestions on how to manipulate the soil economically when searching for Government Corners.

The remarks on retracement of lines and the restoration of "Lost and Obliterated Corners" is treated more fully than usual. The subdivision of sections, and especially of fractional sections, and the method of locating the 1-16 section corners of the fractional half miles is given special attention as it is by many surveyors the least understood and in practice the most abused to the injury of the land holder.

There is added a table of latitudes for each mile north from the *Base*, and for each Standard Parallel, and a table showing the length of a degree of longitude in chains and miles on each Standard Parallel.

Respectfully submitted,

ROBERT HARVEY, State Surveyor.

GENERAL LAWS

Law providing for settlement of grievances or disputes growing out of conflicting surveys of lands or lots. R. S. page 5560.

SECTION 5563. The commissioner of public lands and buildings shall appoint a competent and experienced land surveyor, who shall also be a competent draughtsman, who shall be known and designated as the "State Surveyor and Draughtsman" to take charge under the supervision of the commissioner of public lands and buildings, of the field notes, maps, charts, and records of the United States surveys, and to perform such other duties as may be prescribed by the commissioner of public lands and buildings. *Provided, further*, that the commissioner of public lands and buildings may, when in his judgment there is need of expediting settlement of the disputes referred to in Section 9522 of Cobbey's Annotated Statutes for 1907, appoint one or more competent and experienced deputy land surveyors, each of whom shall make such surveys as may be assigned him, and report his work together with all the necessary notes and maps to the commissioner of public lands and buildings. Upon approval of his report and accompanying documents by the commissioner of public lands and buildings, the same shall be used in all respects as though made by the chief state surveyor and draughtsman. Each deputy appointed under the provisions of this act shall be entitled to five dollars per day and necessary expenses for the time actually engaged in service, to be paid by the parties interested in any disputes over surveys or boundaries.

SEC. 6564. The commissioner of public lands and buildings shall refer to the said surveyor all questions or inquiries relating to surveys, grievances or disputes growing out of conflicting surveys of lands or lots. Said Surveyor and Draughtsman shall issue and prepare the advice, instruction and opinion and issue the same under the approval of the commissioner of public lands and buildings. In case a survey is petitioned for, he shall perform that duty and report the same with the necessary notes and maps to the commissioner of public lands and buildings, and when said notes and maps are so approved and filed and recorded in the office of the county surveyor of the county in which the survey was had, shall be prima facie evidence of the correctness thereof. And it shall be the duty of the said county surveyor to record and file said notes and maps in the county surveyor's records of the county in which the survey is made.

Provided. Any person or persons having an interest in the lands affected by such survey may appeal therefrom in the manner provided by law. He shall also prepare and issue under the authority and direction of the said commissioner of public lands and buildings, a circular of instructions to the county surveyors of the state, for their direction and guidance, in the restoration and establishment of lines and preservation of corners in conformity with the laws, rules and regulations governing the surveys of the United States, and established rules of surveying; and for the concise and comprehensive preparation and recording of field notes and maps of surveys. He shall also perform such other duties as the commissioner of public lands and buildings may require.

SEC. 6565. There shall be paid to the state treasurer for each day the said surveyor is necessarily absent from the office in making any survey, the sum of six dollars per day for the services of said surveyor, and the necessary expenses incurred in making the same. All such fees so received to be paid into the state treasury for the use of the general fund of the state.

SEC. 4. In case of any dispute among owners of land arising for or by reason of any survey of boundaries of lands within this state, or, in case of dispute or disagreement between surveyors as to said surveys or boundaries, the same shall be referred to the said "State Surveyor and Draughtsman" for settlement, and he is hereby appointed as arbitrator to settle and determine such disputes or dis-agreements as to said surveys and boundaries, and whose decision shall be prima facie evidence of the correctness thereof. There shall be paid to the state treasurer for the services of the said state surveyor and draughtsman in settling and disposing of the said disputes and differences the sum of six dollars per day for each day's services actually performed by the said surveyor and draughtsman, to be paid by the parties directly interested in the said con-troversy and said survey or said boundaries and said sum or sums of money so received therefrom shall be paid into the state treasury for the benefit of the general fund of the state.

All acts in conflict repealed. Approved April 8, 1903. In force July 9, 1903.

PENALTY FOR ALTERING OR REMOVING LANDMARKS, CORNERS, OR BEARING TREES

3003. SEC. 150. *Destroying bridges and landmarks.* If any person shall knowingly, willfully and maliciously demolish, cut down or destroy any private, public or toll bridge, cut, fell, deface, alter or remove any landmark, corner or bearing tree, properly established, the person so offending shall be fined in any sum not exceeding five hundred dollars, or imprisoned in the jail of the county not exceeding thirty days, or both. (G. S. p. 743; Ann. 2171; Comp. 7756.) R. S. 3003.

IMITATION OF GOVERNMENT CORNERS

8717. SEC. 142. *Imitation government corners* – It shall be unlawful for any civil engineer, county surveyor, private surveyor, "locator," or any other person, to establish or perpetuate any corner in imitation of corners established by the government of the United States in the survey of the public lands of Nebraska, by digging "quadrangular trenches" and "witness pits," or "witness pits" in either dimension, distance or direction, as adopted by the general land office at Washington, D. C., and practiced by the United States deputy surveyors in the surveys of the public lands of Nebraska. (1913 p. 150.)

8718. SEC. 143 *Violation – penalty* – Any person or persons violating the provisions of the last preceding section shall, upon conviction thereof, be fined in any sum not less than ten dollars nor more than fifty dollars for each and every violation thereof, and in addition thereto be liable for any and all damages to the party or parties caused by said wrongful act. (1913 p. 151.)

Approved April 3, 1913.

PENALTIES FOR DESTROYING CORNER MONUMENTS

To aid in the protection of all evidences of Public Land Surveys, the following law was enacted as a clause in Chapter

398, 29 United States Statutes at Large, page 343, which was approved June 10, 1896:

Provided further, That hereafter it shall be unlawful for any person to destroy, deface, change or remove to another place any section corner, quarter-section corner, or meander post, on any Government line of survey, or to cut down any witness tree, or any tree blazed to mark the line of a Government survey, or to deface, change, or remove any monument or bench mark of any Government survey. That any person who shall offend against any of the provisions of this paragraph shall be deemed guilty of a misdemeanor, and upon conviction thereof, in any court shall be fined not exceeding two hundred and fifty dollars, or be imprisoned not more than one hundred days. All the fines accruing under this paragraph shall be paid into the Treasury and the informer in each case of conviction shall be paid the sum of twenty-five dollars.

OFFICE OF COMMISSIONER OF PUBLIC LANDS AND BUILDINGS,

LINCOLN, NEBRASKA, March 16, 1914.

This Office is in continual receipt of inquiries from county surveyors throughout the state as to the proper method of executing the perplexing duties they are often called upon to perform.

The increasing demand for information, as well as the recently enacted law, has rendered necessary the preparation of this Second Edition of the Circular of Instructions to the county surveyors of the state, which is based upon the spirit of the Acts of Congress authorizing and governing the survey of the Public Domain, the construction placed upon them by the General Land Office, the decisions of the courts and established rules of surveying.

Every person before attempting to perform the duties of surveyor, should have a thorough knowledge of the manner in which the Public Lands were divided into Ranges, Townships, Sections, and the law governing the subdivision of sections into their legal subdivisions, and the "Restoration of Lost or Obliterated Corners" of the Government surveys.

The earlier system of establishing closing corners of section lines, closing on Township lines, causing double corners, and of closing corners of section lines of contiguous Ranges, causing triple corners on the Range lines does not seem to have been carried into Nebraska surveys, excepting the closing corners on the Parallels or Correction Lines, Indian Reservations and State Boundaries, and in the resurvey of certain townships in Western Nebraska between the years of 1894 and 1901.

THE BASE LINE

An arc of the 40th Parallel of North Latitude is the Kansas-Nebraska *Base Line*. The Initial Point was established on the west bank of the Missouri River by Capt. Thos. J. Lee of the U. S. A. in October, 1854, and the line was extended west to the summit of the Rocky Mountains, but on the admission of the Territory as a state into the Union in 1867, the west boundary was limited to the 25th deg. of Longitude west from Washington.

THE PRINCIPAL MERIDIAN

The Sixth Principal Meridian which governs the system of numbering the Ranges in Nebraska, extends from the

Kansas-Nebraska, or Base Line, north to the Missouri River and crosses the Union Pacific R. R. immediately west of Columbus in Platte County. Ranges east of this line to the Missouri River are designated as Range No. .... east, and Ranges west to the Colorado and Wyoming Line as Range No. .... west of the Sixth Principal Meridian.

STANDARD PARALLELS

Standard Parallels were run *east* from the 6th Principal Meridian to the Missouri River and *west* to west boundary of the state along the north boundary of every 4th township or every 24th mile from the Kansas-Nebraska line to check errors in measurement and the accumulation of convergencies of Meridians. They are numbered from 1 to 8 consecutively.

GUIDE MERIDIANS

To check the accumulation of errors of measurements a Guide Meridian was run from the 48th Mile Post on the Base Line, and east of the 6th Principal Meridian, North without offsets for convergency to the north Boundary, and west of the 6th Principal Meridian from every 48th Mile Post, Guide Meridians were run north to the north Boundary, offsetting for convergency on each Standard Parallel, and are numbered from 1 to 7 consecutively.

All meridians east and west converge towards the Principal Meridian from the equator to the poles, and at any given point from the equator the distance between any two meridians is less than at the equator.

RANGE LINES

Range lines, *east* or *west* of the Principal Meridian were run from every 6th Mile Post on the Base Line, north to the north Boundary, offsetting for convergency on each Standard Parallel, and converge towards the 6th Principal Meridian.

TOWNSHIP LINES

Township lines were run east and west every 6th Mile of Latitude from the Base Line.

For every township or six miles of latitude, the convergence of range lines towards the Meridian, averages 62 links from Latitude 40 to the 41 deg.; 64 links from Latitude 41 to 42 deg.; and 66½ links from Latitude 42 to 43 deg.

The north line of the township is therefore, theoretically, the same length as the south lines, less the amount of convergency for the six miles of latitude. This explains why the western tier of sections in every township is fractional, the deficiency increasing from south to north through all of the townships.

Townships are numbered 1 to 35 consecutively from the Base Line to the North Boundary.

DESIGNATION OF CORNERS

Half mile and mile corners established on Standard Parallels are the initial points for surveys on the north side of the line and are known as Standard ¼ Section Corners and Standard Section Corners; every 6th mile corner is also designated a Standard Township Corner.

The 24th mile corner of each Guide Meridian and all corners established at the intersection of lines run from the south to the Standard Parallels or lines intersecting Military

Position of Corner Mound common to four Townships or four Sections

Plan

N

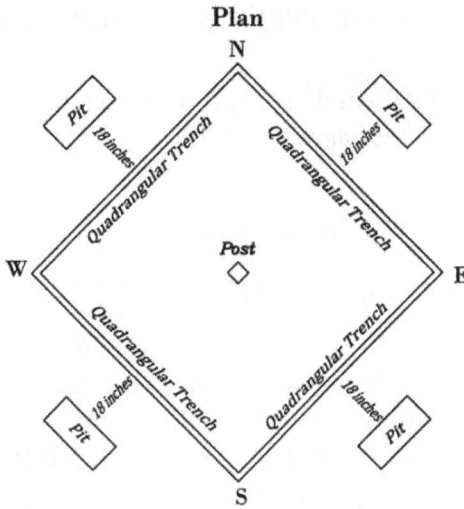

W   E

S

Fig. 4

Position of Corner Mound common to two Townships or two Sections

Plan

N

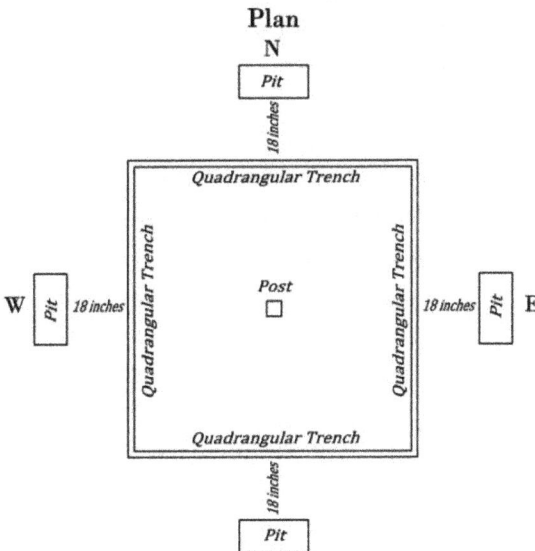

Fig. 5.

or Indian Reservations and the state lines are called *Closing Corners.*

Corners established at the intersection of lakes and rivers are called *Meander Corners.*

REGARDING METHODS OF PERPETUATING THE ORIGINAL SITUS OF GOVERNMENT CORNERS IN NEBRASKA

An examination of the field notes of the Government surveys in this state, shows that the material usually employed to perpetuate the exact corner point was a stake or post set or driven into the ground, a stone, charcoal or charred stake; and when trees were found growing in the vicinity they were usually marked and recorded as witnesses. In the open prairie country a quadrangular trench a foot wide and a foot deep was dug around the corner and the earth piled up along the outer edge of the trench; rectangular pits, 24 x 18 x 12 inches or two feet square were dug outside and opposite each of the four sides of the trench, and the earth piled up around the post in a conical mound. After a few years, the "trench" was discarded in the early history of the surveys, but the "pit" was retained as a witness in all the future surveys in the state.

It is noted however, as an exception to the last remark that in *some* counties where stone abounded, this material was used to mark the location of the corners, without digging either trench or pits, for witnesses, and unfortunately the notes of these surveys were approved and the work accepted; for it is the experience of all surveyors that when a stone or stake is used for a monument, without witnesses or a suitable enduring memorial being separately placed alongside or beneath, and the monument is removed by accident or design, the exact location of the corner is liable to be forever lost.

A *stake* or *post* driven into the ground without an enduring memorial placed at the foot of the post or alongside, is always open to the suspicion of it having been placed there by some one either by accident or design and for a different purpose than the perpetuation of the original corner.

MEMORIALS PLACED IN CORNERS

Charcoal. Most surveyors and land owners, generally understand that charcoal was used to perpetuate the corners of the public surveys and therefore they dig and search for charcoal expecting to find it in considerable quantities or in large lumps. The rules specified *Charcoal*, but when it was used in bulk, it is observed that the field notes frequently mention a *pint* as the quantity deposited, and no doubt a lesser quantity was often deposited, more or less pulverized. The field notes show that in the western part of the state where timber was very scarce, there are many townships where the surveyors did not deposit any charcoal or other memorial in the corners. Fine charcoal in course of time disintegrates and assimilates with the soil, loses its characteristics as to form and color by reason of dampness, freezing and thawing, and admixture with the soil; so it is frequently found as having the appearance of a deposit of soil and ashes dropped into a crevice or cavity; or the outline of the edge or border of the deposit of pulverized coal may have become shaded down by its assimilation with the surrounding soil so as to deceive an experienced surveyor as to its real identity. It does not often occur that charcoal in considerable quantities, or in lumps large enough to be easily seen, is found even by experienced surveyors, so that "digging for corners" by inexperienced persons is a very dangerous experiment.

Charred Stake. Whatever may have been the intention of the Department in denominating a "Charred Stake" as a suitable memorial for corners, it is evident that at an early period it caused uncertainty and confusion; for in the experience of local and county surveyors, it has been found that a short round piece of charred wood was often deposited alongside or at the foot of the post; at other times it would be the sharpened end of the post itself that was charred, so we find a U. S. Deputy Surveyor writing to his Surveyor General requesting definite information on the subject. The subsequent method practiced by the Deputy as appears from the evidence in the field shows that the method of charring the sharpened end of the post for a "Charred Stake" had at least the tacit sanction of the Supervising Office. Therefore the expression "Charred Stake" found in the first and subsequent Manuals issued by the General Land Office, and in the field notes, may, according to an established custom, refer to a short piece of charred wood lying at the foot or driven alongside of the post, or to the sharpened and charred end of the post itself.

REGARDING METHODS PRACTICED IN ESTABLISHING GOVERNMENT CORNERS

From the statements of the U. S. Deputy Surveyors still living, corroborated by the evidence discovered by careful and experienced surveyors, it is evident that in the establishment of government lines, it was the practice of the cornermen after the alignment of the corner by the compassman, to dig a hole with his spade, either rectangular or square, and from six inches to a foot in depth, at the designated point, and set a post therein and deposit the charcoal or "Charred Stake" alongside; or if the post was *sharpened* and *charred*, that would be driven instead, or it might be, as was frequently the case, the formality of digging a hole was dispensed with and the sharpened post driven into the sod. When a *square hole* was dug, it was usually about seven inches wide, or the width of the spade and from six to twelve inches deep. When rectangular they were made with four cuts of the spade; the side cuts sloped toward each other and were cut off at each end forming a wedge shaped sod about seven inches long by five or six inches wide by eight or ten deep and easily removed from its place. In the hole thus formed the post was set, charcoal deposited or the sharpened charred post driven; when in position the pits were dug and the earth therefrom piled up around the post. These pits were intended for witnesses to the corner and varied in dimensions from eighteen inches to three feet square according to the kind of corner. Their direction and distance from the post varied also according to the kind of corner, but generally, however, according to the method first learned by the deputy surveyors, but the direction was almost invariably according to the following specifications:

1. Section corners on Standard Parallels, three pits, N. E. and W. of corner.

2. ¼ Section corners on Standard Parallels, two pits – E. and W. of corner.

3. Section corners on Township or Subdivisional lines, four pits either N. S. E. and W. of corner or diagonally, a pit in each section.

4. ¼ Section corners on Township or Subdivisional lines, sometimes four pits, N. S. E. and W. when so dug, the pits at the section corners were dug diagonally, one in each section.

5. After 1868 or 1869, ¼ section corners had two pits, either dug *on line* one on each side of the corner, or across the line, a pit in each section. The distance the pits were dug from the corner varied from three to ten feet, but more generally from five to seven feet. The distance and direction would generally be quite uniform in each deputy's contract, but they might differ in another and adjacent contract, or where two or more deputies were joint contractors and worked jointly in the same Township.

This lack of uniformity in many of the details such as above mentioned was owing to the department not having established specific rules and enforced strict compliance by the deputies until 1881, when the surveys of the state were nearly completed.

NOTE – In 1869 the Surveyor General verbally instructed his deputies or some of them at least, to dig two pits at ¼ sec. cor. and across the line, one in each section, and four at section corners – one in each section. However, some deputies continued to dig four pits at ¼ section corners as late as 1874. (See Garfield County.)

THE GRADUAL OBLITERATION OF CORNERS

When the Government surveys were first executed the corners established were prominent landmarks, but in course of time the mounds of earth were worn down by the action of the winds and storms, the posts knocked down by wild beasts, buffalo, elk, antelope, etc., or pulled up and carried away by Indians and white men (which very often happened.) In such cases the only evidence of the corner point remaining would be the mark or outline of the hole dug by the cornermen, and the memorial deposited therein.

In many instances the hewed sides of the sharpened end of the post were not deeply charred, only smoked, but in all probability the point was thoroughly burned, and should such a post be removed, the extreme point was liable to be broken off, to remain in the ground, a minute memorial to faintly mark the exact spot. Should it be that the sharpened and charred post rotted off, leaving the point in the ground, the wooded part would decay and return to dust leaving a charred shell, sometimes as thin as paper, tipped at the lower end with a solid piece of charcoal; again it often occurred that posts were used without being charred, and without a deposit of charcoal; or the charcoal may have been so finely pulverized as to easily assimilate and mix with the surrounding soil, or the soil so black as to render it undistinguishable.

Again it may have been that the entire post was carried away, leaving the hole to be filled with earth or a sediment of different color and texture, forming a core easily recognized. It may be, when stone was used for corners, the surveyor by due care, will find the stone removed and the hole where it stood now filled with a different soil, or sediment with a few small spalls of the stone. In any and all cases the most careful manipulation and closest scrutiny by an *experienced* surveyor is necessary to prevent the loss of this valuable evidence.

The Value of Government Field Notes in the Retracement of Original Surveys

The discrepancies between remeasurements of the original lines, and the distances stated in the Government Field Notes, causes many surveyors to discredit the value of these notes, and declare them worthless.

The government enacted laws as to how the Public Lands should be surveyed and for the sale thereof. The lands were conveyed according to that survey. The monuments established on the ground by the surveyors constitute the survey and whenever and wherever found they mark the boundaries of the land conveyed; this law is not only upheld but emphasized by many decisions of the Supreme, State and Federal Courts. The latest by our Supreme Court is the notable case of "The State of Nebraska vs. Ball" 93 Neb. 358. In this case the corner found by the court to be the original, or Government corner, is more than 32 chains or 128 rods from where it should have been.

The notation of creeks, ravines, and other natural objects by the surveyor are data to assist in locating the position of corners. Lost and obliterated corners are to be restored according to the best evidence of their original position, and very often the field notes furnish the best and most conclusive evidence and the recorded length of the lines is the basis for equitable distribution of excesses or deficiencies of remeasurements.

The surveyor who ignores Government corners and makes new ones, or ignores the field notes, in the absence of better evidence, will soon find himself in disrepute, in contempt of court decisions and subject to impeachment.

Government corners cannot be changed.

SHORT CUT METHOD

The Government surveyors braved many dangers, endured great hardships and suffered many privations, which can be appreciated only by those who have engaged in similar service. Many of the surveys were honestly executed and will favorably compare with surveys performed under less trying circumstances; but for surveys executed with a careless and dishonest intent there is little excuse. However, since the Government made the surveys while it was the owner of the land, and disposed of the lands according to the monuments established by the Deputy Surveyor, the surveyor cannot ignore them even if not found where strict professional care would have placed them.

In the early history of our rectangular system of Public Surveys, the Government Surveyors discovered a shorter method of executing the surveys in the field, than that prescribed by the Rules and Regulations; and in Ohio, Indiana, Michigan, Wisconsin, Minnesota, Illinois and Iowa, we hear complaints of crooked lines, especially those running East and West, and long and short half miles, causing great differences in area of subdivision in the same section. The method traveled westward with the surveys and crossed the Missouri River into Nebraska.

An explanation of this "short cut" method will throw a great deal of light on the mystery of so many crooked lines and long and short half miles, especially of east and west miles, that has baffled the ingenuity of surveyors to solve.

The Rules provided that the deputy begin the survey of the township at the corner of secs. 35 and 36 on the township line, and run north between secs. 35 and 36, establish the ¼ sec. cor. at 40 chains as he advanced, and at 80 chains establish the section corner. Then, to run east on a random line, set a temporary ¼ sec. cor. at 40 chains and at the intersection of the eastern boundary of the township note the length of the line and the distance from the point of intersection to the section corner; then calculate a course which would run a true line back to the point of starting; on his return establish the ¼ sec. cor. at a point half way, and on line with the section corners; then run north between sections 25 and 26 repeating the operation as before until the lines of the entire eastern tier of six sections were established. The succeeding tiers, were to be established in like manner until the subdivision of the township was completed.

The "short cut" method consisted in this: when the deputy had established the corner of sections 25, 26, 35 and 36, he would run east between sections 25 and 36, 40.00 chains, *only*; here the cornerman would establish the permanent ¼ sec. cor. and the party return to the section corner, and run north between section 25 and 26, then east between sections 24 and 25 and establish the ¼ cor. as before at 40 chains and so continue the work until the ¼ sec. cors. on all of the random lines were established. Now it might be that if the country traversed was reasonably smooth and the day not too far advanced the surveyor would run west from the corner of 1, 2, 11 and 12, his last interior section corner, and establish the corner of sections 2, 3, 10 and 11; then run north half a mile, establish the ¼ sec. cor. and return, and run south to the corner of sections 10, 11, 14 and 15; then run east half a mile to the ¼ sec. cor. and return to camp.

The next morning he would return to the corner of secs. 10, 11, 14 and 15 and run south establishing ¼ sec. cors. on the east lines and between secs. 34 and 35; then from the corner sections 26, 27, 34 and 35, run west one mile and run south half a mile; then return and run north between sections 27 and 28; then east 40.00 chains, then return to the sec. cor. and run north half a mile to the ¼ sec. cor. between sections 21 and 22.

On the third day he would probably commence at the corner of sections 14, 15, 22 and 23 and run west one mile, then north establishing ¼ sec. cors. on the east and west lines, until he reached the township line, thence east on said line 40.00 chains; then return and run west between sections 4 and 33, then south to the corner of sections 8, 9, 16 and 17.

On the fourth day he might begin on the township line and run north between sections 32 and 33, proceeding in a similar manner as on the former days as indicated by the black lines in the diagram.

Instead of beginning the survey of the Township as provided by law, he has been known to have begun not only on the north, east and west boundaries and operate as described, but to establish the township and range lines at the same time and in the same manner as the subdivisional lines as indicated in the diagram. This method of subdividing townships into sections was practiced in a very early period in the history of Government surveys, as far east as central Ohio, at least, and in Michigan, Indiana, Illinois and Iowa before it crossed the Missouri River into Nebraska. Each random line measured only half way, saved one mile of travel, and in the whole township from twenty to twenty-five miles, or two days work. This saving of time was forced upon many of the surveyors by having to pay a per cent of the profits toward campaign expenses.

To illustrate the foregoing explanation, the following figure representing a township where the original corners have since been determined and the bearings and measurements of the mile and half mile lines ascertained by actual retracements. The miles and half miles *actually run and measured* are represented by the solid black lines and the half miles *not measured* by broken lines.

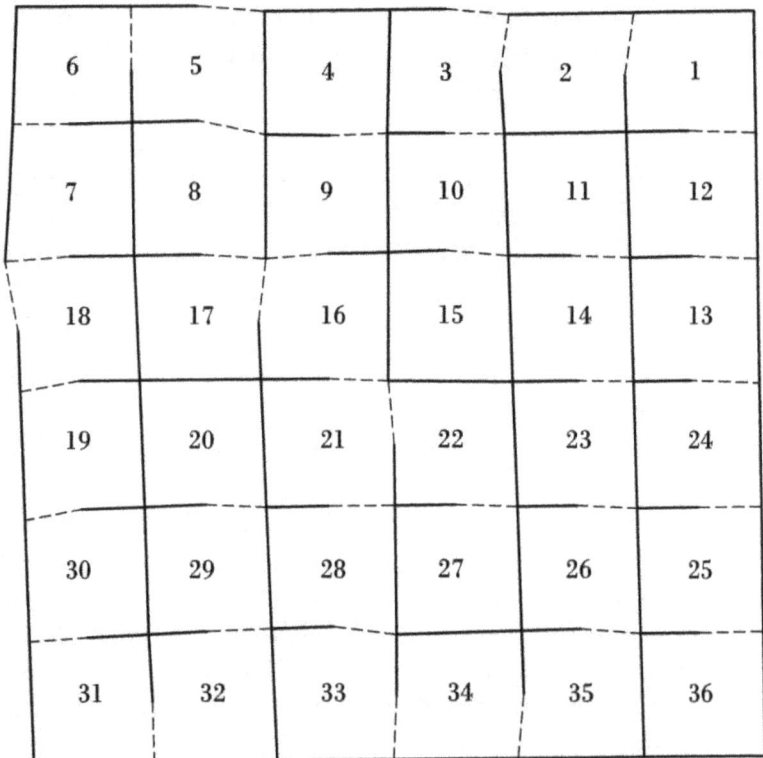

6	5	4	3	2	1
7	8	9	10	11	12
18	17	16	15	14	13
19	20	21	22	23	24
30	29	28	27	26	25
31	32	33	34	35	36

Fig. 1.

By reference to the above Figure, it will be seen that the ¼ sec. cor. between sections 21 and 22 is not connected with the corner of sections 15, 16, 21 and 22 established on the third day's work; and in order to join the two corners the county surveyor must make a sharp deflection from the ¼ sec. cor. to the left in order to reach the sec. cor.

This will explain why it frequently occurs that a serious "break" or "jog" exist in north and south lines.

From what has been said in reference to this "short cut" method of surveying a township, we draw several conclusions:

1. On all lines not wholly run and measured, the two half miles will be of unequal lengths and the ¼ sec. cor. will not be on a straight line with the section corners, except by accident.

2. The half miles actually measured will approximate 40.00 chains, and the half miles not measured will be considerably longer or shorter.

3. The direction of the half miles actually measured will approximate *east* and *west*, or *north* and *south*, while those not measured will have a considerable deflection from the general direction to reach the succeeding corner.

4. The topographical features, such as creeks, canyons, ravines, rocks, etc., noted by the deputy surveyor on the measured half miles, will generally be fairly correct, but on those not measured they will be grossly incorrect or not given at all.

5. The direction of half miles actually run being approximately *east* and *west*, or *north* and *south*, may often be determined by taking the bearings of the roads, fences, hedge lines, etc., of both half miles.

It is hoped that the foregoing explanation of a method of executing many of the government surveys from an early day until recent years, will be of material assistance to many surveyors, who by giving attention to the preceding remarks and applying them to the observations he has made in the field, and a study of the notes of retracements of the original surveys, should be able to determine the method practiced by the deputy in executing the surveys in his county, and with reasonable certainty anticipate his each successive movement.

LOST AND OBLITERATED CORNERS

"An obliterated corner is one where no *visible evidence* remains of the work of the original surveyor in establishing it."

Its location may however, have been preserved beyond all question by acts of the land owners, and by the memory of those who knew and recollect the true *situs* of the original monuments. In such cases it is not a lost corner.

"A lost corner is one whose position cannot be determined beyond reasonable doubt, either from original marks or reliable external evidence." (General Land Office Circular, June 1, 1909.)

REMARKS ON SEARCHING FOR GOVERNMENT CORNERS

It is the fault of many surveyors to treat corners as *lost* whose existence is not readily found on the surface or after a brief and careless search, when in fact every source of information that will afford a clue should be carefully examined, and every statement made by persons who knew the corner when it could be plainly seen, should be fairly considered.

It often occurs that a careful settler has planted a tree, fence post or hedge, with particular reference to the corner in question; or in the open prairie country in an early day, he broke the first furrows of his fields to the corner, or his fire guards on the boundary line of the statutory road limit, or plowed a single furrow from the quarter post to divide his quarter section from that of his neighbor. The roots of the old tree may be found, the hole where the fence post stood is probably still there, the marks of the old hedge may yet exist, and strange as it may seem, the outline of the old furrow may be detected by the very shallow depression of the furrow and the slightly elevated ridge alongside, but more easily by the difference in the color or shading of the grass; and the surveyor should inquire into the matter of who did these things, the habits of carefulness and probable intentions.

Though the exact spot where the corner existed is not known, yet by evidence it may be shown where it stood within certain limits.

Having determined from the appearance of the surface of the ground or other source of information, the approximate location of the missing corner, the surveyor should remove the loose or drifted soil for a considerable space around, to enable him to conveniently work, and to satisfy himself as to the level of the original sod, which may sometimes be done by a comparison with the surrounding surface, or by the appearance of the layers of earth, or occasionally by the thin sheet of black ashes, left by the last of the prairie fires, or by the crowns of the old grass roots; then carefully shave the surface of the ground with a clean sharp spade, removing the soil, in thin layers, so as to present a

Original S. W. corner section 35, T. 19 N., R. 5 W., Boone County. Claimed to be *lost*. Stone with + set for new cor. in resurvey 3 ft. east, cost St. Edward nearly $200 and lot of demolished concrete walks. Original cor. recovered with charcoal deposit and witness pits. Recovered by Robert Harvey, state surveyor, June 26, 1907.

Original ¼ cor. between sections 34 and 35, T. 19 N., R. 5 W. Claimed to be *lost*. In resurveys new corners set a concrete brick and white cedar post with iron rod. Original corner at card at foot of rod. White cards mark the center of the 4 original pits. Recovered by Robert Harvey, State Surveyor, June, 1907.

clean, smooth surface, so that any difference in the formation of the soil, discoloration or foreign substance may be seen. It may be necessary to go over the ground several times in order to reach the level of any deposits or marks made by the Deputy Surveyor. If a small quantity of pulverized charcoal was thrown loosely into the hole marking the corner point it would in all probability be so reduced in thickness as to form a thin deposit, likely to escape detection, unless the soil is carefully removed in thin layers or sheets, sometimes even to the sixteenth of an inch or less in thickness.

By exercising due care, the surveyor may, where stone was used for corners, find small spalls of stone and the hole where the stone had been set now filled with a different soil or sediment.

But in the open prairie country where posts were used, he may find a substantial piece of charred wood, a good sized lump of charcoal, or more generally fine charcoal intermixed with the soil, giving it a darker color in which the particles of coal cannot be seen without the aid of a magnifying glass; or the deposit may have a speckled appearance, the particles of coal being large enough to be seen, or the decayed post may be found reduced to a pulp and filled with grass roots, or to a fine dry dust, so that a tally or marking pin will drop or be easily thrust to the bottom; by cutting a cross section at one side of the hole a full and clear outline of the size and shape of the original post may be seen, and perhaps, if the post was charred, the sides may be a thin blackened shell or crust of charcoal, tipped at the lower end with a small piece of coal.

It may be, however, that the post with its charred point

has been pulled out, and the only remaining evidence of the actual corner is the cavity filled with fallen sand or fine dust presenting a deposit or core somewhat similar to the shape of the post, or the shape of the hole dug by the cornermen in which the post was set or driven, and may be identified by the clean cut sides and the different color and density of the material filling the hole.

Often newer posts or stakes are driven until several are found, each one claiming to mark the original corner, yet all differing from a few inches to several feet. The surveyor will have little difficulty in deciding which is the original post or stake, by its appearance, it being more completely decayed, and generally of a darker color.

It may be said that as a rule the original post or stake was cut from green round timber and driven down straight with the bark on. The work being done from day to day by the same set of men will have a uniformity of appearance, while stakes driven by other surveyors or settlers, of soft and hard woods differing from the native timber, indifferently sharpened, and usually with a dull ax, will be driven in a slanting direction.

There is in the whole appearance of corners established by U. S. Deputy Surveyors, in their respective contracts, such a degree of uniformity in the kind of timber, the method of sharpening, charring, setting or driving posts, digging of the holes to receive them, deposits of memorials, decay of the wooded portions and preservation by nature's process, as to stamp it with a degree of truthfulness that will seldom mislead the experienced surveyor; yet he should not wholly trust to the appearance of the corner itself in making up his conclusions, but endeavor to corroborate the same, by

Outline of the S. W. pit of original corner, Blaine County, Nebraska. Established July 29, 1872, in sandy soil. Deposit is drifted black prairie ashes, sand and dust. Color, gray. Loaned by N. B. Sweitzer, Ass't Supervisor U. S. Surveys in Nebraska.

the extrinsic evidence of witness trees, trenches or pits, and connection by course and measurement with other known corners.

EVIDENCE OF WITNESS TREES, TRENCH AND PITS

Where recourse is had to witness trees to find the corner, it will be generally found that those taken by the Deputy Surveyors have been destroyed, but the indications of an old stump or depression in the ground may be found and by cutting away the sod with a sharp spade the crown of the stump roots may be laid bare or roots leading to the stump be found, and a skillful woodsman will not only recognize the kind of wood but the direction of the stump as well. If two or more trees have been recorded and the bearings and distances disagree, some of the bearings or distances may be wrong; or the average bearing or distance, or both, may indicate the actual spot.

Witness Trench. In the early surveys the quadrangular trench was understood to be a "spade deep" and dug with the sides diagonally at corners common to four townships or four sections, and to face the cardinal points at corners common to two townships or two sections and the ¼ section corners, outside of these and about 18 inches from the middle of each side of the trench, the pit was dug.

Before the surveys of the State had progressed very far the trench was abandoned. Therefore what is said under the subject of *witness pits* will apply to the trench and pits.

Witness Pits. Very few of the county and local surveyors appreciate the great importance of the *witness pits* and the necessity of preserving them with as little mutilation as possible. It is generally understood that when their appearance on the surface has disappeared, their identity is lost. *This is a great mistake*, as will be readily conceded when it is explained that probably within a few months after these witness pits were dug, prairie fires swept over the country, followed by high winds that sifted and eddied the ashes and particles of burned grass stems into the pits, succeeded by rains and snows and drifting dust and sand, followed the next year by the same process, continually filling the holes which gradually grew wider by the sloughing off of the sides by the action of the rains, snows, thawing and freezing, until finally in the long course of years they have become almost obliterated, leaving perhaps only slight depressions covered over with grass; but pits dug as far back as 1870 are very generally covered up, especially where their location is subject to wash or overflow, but in tolerably flat and hard ground, they may still be readily seen; when the prairie fires ceased to sweep over the prairies, the holes began filling with other and lighter colored material.

Though the surveyor may feel reasonably certain that he has found the original corner, yet he should fortify his conclusions by laying bare the evidences of these original witness pits.

Knowing the general direction of the pits from the corners in his county, he can measure off the general distance and carefully remove the sod or loose soil from a piece of ground say 5 or 6 feet in diameter, then gently shave the earth with a clean sharp spade until he comes upon an irregular circle of black ashes intermingled with soil or sand, which marks the period when the prairie fires ceased; the circle may be 25 or 30 inches in diameter, but on going down, being careful to keep the surface continually flat, he will observe that the deposit will probably grow darker, the outer edge generally much the darkest until he reaches the bottom, which will in all probability be dark or black all over; the diameter of the circle will have grown less until it now approximates the measurement of the original pit and may have a rectangular or square form with rounded corners. All of the pits should be fully exposed to complete the evidence for the Surveyors' Record, and satisfaction to the adjacent and interested land owners, who have a right to the explanation of the process of preserving the identity of the pits and to know by personal observation at the time, that the evidences agreed with the explanations given before the ground is opened. Sometimes, and we may say more generally it is easier and safer to search for the pits first, or for all at the same time by clearing off the ground for 20-30 or more feet square, removing the sod and loose earth in thin slices, then going over the ground with sharp spades, being careful to keep the surface even, carefully observing every difference in the soil or foreign substance, especially for pieces of charcoal or decayed wood or mark of the hole the post had left. When the surface is fairly smooth a good mould board plow with a sharp share can be safely and economically employed in turning over the sod to a depth of two or three inches in prairie sod, or to the bottom of the furrows of cultivated land. If the plow share is kept filed to a smooth sharp edge and held flat with the surface, so as to cut a sharp, clean furrow, the outline of the pits can generally be readily detected by the difference in color of the deposit. Should the share become dull, or the edge become clogged by fine grass roots so as to blur the sharp outlines, or dust fall back or blow into the furrows it will be necessary to clear the bottom of the furrows with sharp spades or shovels.

NOTE – I have found after long experience that long handle, flat steel shovels are to be preferred to spades as being a labor saver and are less back breaking; the blades should be kept constantly bright and filed to a thin sharp chisel edge. The handles should be cut back to a suitable and convenient length and fitted with nibs.

The original post, whatever may be the indication of its former position, will be found within the limits of the opposite pits and within a reasonable distance of the center. Having found the evidence of the corner and of the witness pits, the surveyor should now perpetuate the corner in the most enduring manner with imperishable material.

The corner may be perpetuated by digging a hole at the corner point 8 to 12 inches square, neat, smooth and clean, two or more feet deep, owing to locality, and deposit coal, cinders, broken earthware, queensware, bottles, etc., set a stone on top and fill around with cinders or different colored earth, or drive a heavy gas pipe or machine shaft, with brick set on end around it. It is a good plan to deposit beneath the stone, or deep in the ground alongside of the pipe or shaft, a hard pressed or paving brick with the description of the corner, the date, by month, day and year, and the surveyor's initials neatly cut thereon with a sharp, narrow chisel.

To perpetuate the pits, bore a hole with a two or two and a half inch auger in the center of each pit two or more feet deep, owing to locality, and fill with slacked lime; then measure with a tape line or flag pole (which is usually

Corner found, Cherry County, Nebraska, and photo taken August 13, 1912. No surface indications. Plow and spades used. Loaned by N. B. Sweitzer, Ass't Supervisor U. S. Surveys in Nebraska.

Outline of east pit of original ¼ standard corner. T. 25 N., R. 22 W., 6th P. M., Brown County, Nebraska. In heavy soil. No surface indications. Corner established August 6, 1872. Loaned by N . B. Sweitzer, Ass't Supervisor U. S. Surveys in Nebraska.

divided into feet and halves) from the corner to the center of the pits thus marked.

During the work of perpetuating the corner the surveyor should carefully and particularly note in his field book each particular kind of material used, giving dimensions if possible, distance and direction to the center of the pits, and be particular to record his notes in the Official Record when he returns home.

We have thus been particular in describing the appearance of a government corner surrounded by its witness pits fully laid bare and exposed after the lapse of many years. We have, however, presented only one phase or picture of this phenomena of nature, of which there are many; for instance, on a steep slope, the traces of the black ashes may be traced down the hill side from the pit for several feet, as though the rains had washed the floating ashes and cinders from the pit down the hill; but this feature will not extend from the pits up hill; among the "cat-steps" or at the foot of a steep bank, a succeeding rain storm may have washed the pit full of yellow clay and will be in contrast with the darker soil in which the pits were dug; or, near the top of a clay hill where the full force of the northwest wind could strike, and where the ashes and cinders could scarcely find lodgment, there the pits would probably be filled with the surface washing from the hill top.

In the sand hill region an entirely different phase is presented. In the valleys the pits will be filled with ashes intermixed with the drifted sand. Very often the body of the deposit in the pits will have a light appearance, while around the edge or margin it will generally be black. Where the surface is more sandy, the deposit is black ashes and drifted white sand intermixed, presenting a gray or lead colored appearance; or if in the sweep of a shortly succeeding sand storm, or over the crest of a denuded sand hill, there, it may be a deposit of white drifted sand.

Along highways, a corner or the side of a pit may be found in the side of the wagon track. In cultivated fields only the bottom of the pits could escape destruction.

The work of unearthing the Original or Government Corners cannot be successfully, or even safely prosecuted while the ground is frozen, as it is impossible to clearly distinguish the difference between the deposit in the pits and the original soil, on account of not being able to shave the ground smoothly, and of the frost crystals causing confusion and uncertainty in detecting the difference in color.

It will therefore be seen that the varied appearance of the evidences and conditions under which these old corners and witness pits are found, requires long practice and close study to render the surveyor capable of determining their genuineness, and the difference between true and bogus corners, or corners made many years after. Surveyors who have spent more than a quarter of a century in the constant practice of retracing Government lines and unearthing all kinds of corners, under many varying conditions by which nature did its work, and every day bringing new conditions and many surprises, are often puzzled and perplexed as to the interpretation to be placed upon certain appearances and conditions.

RETRACEMENT OF LINES

There is one rule which can and *must be* rigidly followed in all cases in restoring lost boundary lines and corners, and

WEST END

Standard cor. Secs. 35 and 36, T. 17 N., R. 14 W., on Greeley-Valley county line, in deep flat ravine; excavation 20'x10'x6' deep through wash from fields.   Original corner found rotten point of post, charcoal, witness pits. Drove 9 foot iron pipe, bottle for memorial, mark original witness pits with lime.   By ROBERT HARVEY, State Surveyor, April, 1911.

East end of same excavation.   Five men ¼ day.   Mark original witness pits with lime. Corner established September 6, 1867.

that is, the surveyor should make every effort to find the exact location of the missing corner or line, and *his aim should be to find where the corner or line was, and not where it ought to be.*

When resort is had to retracement of lines to accomplish this purpose, the *presumption* is that the results will indicate the *probable location* of the lines and corners.

Therefore, in retracements he should be careful to note the distances to all creeks, ravines, sloughs, rocks, trees, etc., that he may compare them with the distances noted in the original field notes, to assist him in identifying the original lines and landmarks. If a government line, it may furnish the conclusive evidence of which half mile was actually run on east and west lines, and on north and south lines where a "break or jog" was made. The proximity of a ravine or slough may point out the location of the corner.

The surveyor should constantly bear in mind that all government lines and corners have a relationship to each other according to a certain plan, and in the retracement of lines the rediscovered portions should be consistent with the plan, or some of the elements of the plan. Every corner has a connection with some other corner by a measured line. A corner not known to be an original corner should neither be approved and endorsed in the record, nor condemned until thorough investigation is made, not only of its appearance, but its relationship by course and measurement with some part of the system. In search for the ¼ section corners on east and west lines, it is important to know which half mile was actually measured, or when a "jog or break" occurred on north and south lines.

How to Restore Lost or Obliterated Corners

The Government has established the law by which lost or obliterated corners are to be restored.

In general, corners established by the Deputy Surveyor at uniform distance (as recorded in the field notes) on Meridians, Standard Parallels, Range and Township lines, being independent and advanced surveys, are supposed to be *straight* lines, and that distances between known government corners are to be divided equally among all the half miles, whether the remeasured distance is more or less than the original distance stated in the field notes.

In all other cases the distance is not to be divided equally, but proportionately.

This will be fully exemplified in the following diagrams and examples.

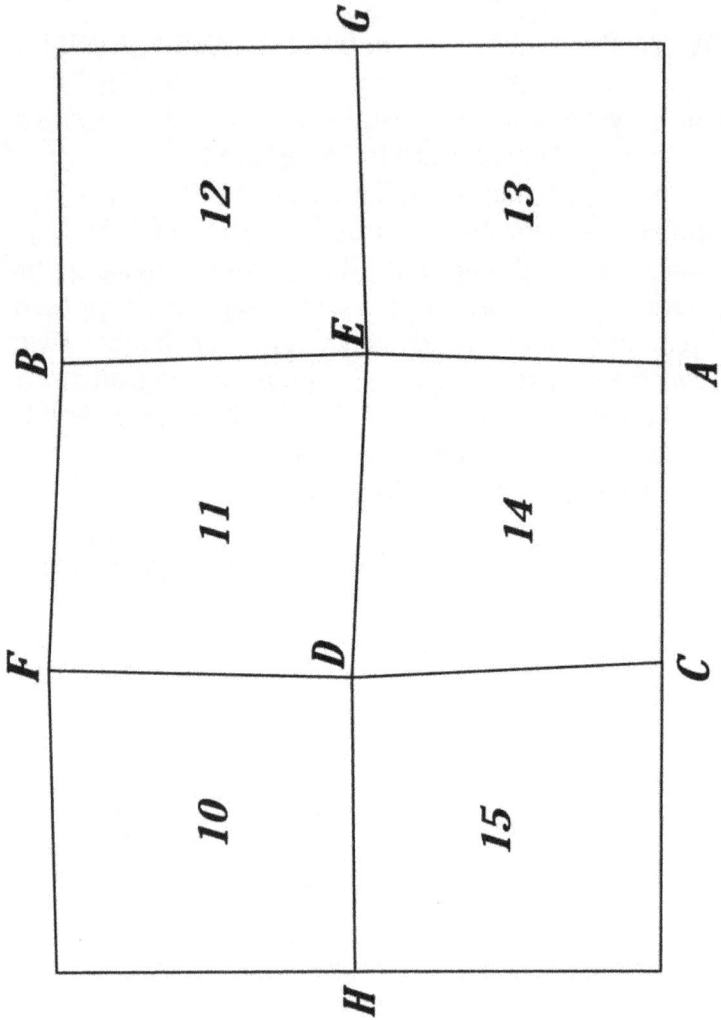

FIGURE 2

Example 1.   Required to restore the section corners at E and D and all the ¼ sec. cors. On the lines designated in Fig. 2.

Method... The Government field notes show that the

north and south miles are of equal length, and that EG is 79.50 chains, ED, 80.50, and HD 80.25, total 240.25 chains. The lengths being unequal, they cannot be established equidistant, but at proportional distances. It is therefore necessary for the county surveyor to measure all of the lines to obtain the data from which to make the necessary calculations to enable him to restore the corners and lines correctly.

We will suppose the measurement of these lines to result as follows, to-wit: AB, 161.00 chains; CF, 159.00 chains, and GH 241.50 chains. The lines between secs. 11 and 12, 13 and 14, will be 80.50 chains, and between secs. 10 and 11, 14 and 15, 79.50 chains each.

To determine the positions of E and D east and west, we have the following proportions:

240.25 : 241.50 : : 79.50 = 79.91 = the true length of the line of EG according to the county surveyor's measurement.

for ED we have,

240.25 : 241.50 : : 80.50 = 80.92 = the true length of ED; for DH,

240.25 : 241.50 : : 80.25 = 80.67 = the true length of DH, and the ¼ sec. cors. will be restored on line and equidistant between their respective section corners.

TO RESTORE THE ¼ SEC. CORS. ON THE NORTH AND WEST FRACTIONAL MILES OF THE TOWNSHIP

Example 2. Required to restore the ¼ sec. cor. between sections 2 and 3.

The Government field note length of the line between sections 2 and 3 is 80.90 chains. By the county surveyor's measurement it is 79.40 chains, then say,

80.90 : 79.40: : 40.00 = 39.258 chains=the true length of the south half mile; and 79.40 – 39.26 = 40.14 chains = the length of the north half mile.

The ¼ sec. cors. on the west fractional miles of the Township are restored in precisely the same manner.

HOW TO RESTORE CLOSING CORNERS OF LINES CLOSING ON THE PARALLELS OR BOUNDARY LINES

Example 3.   Required to restore the closing corner of a Range Line between sections 1 and 6 on the Parallel or Boundary Line.

Method. The closing corner of a Range Line between sections 1 and 6 was established according to the field notes, 10.70 chains east of the ¼ sec. cor. on the south boundary of section 31.

The length of each half mile on the Parallel is 40.00 chains, original measurement, and the Closing Corner is supposed to have been established on a *straight line* between the nearest Standard section and ¼ section corners.

By the county surveyor's measurement the distance from the ¼ sec. cor. to the corner of sections 31 and 32, is 40.25 chains:

then,

40.00 : 40.25 : : 10.70 = 10.77 chains, the true distance from the ¼ sec. cor. east to the point where the corner is to be restored. (General Land Office Circular on "Lost and Obliterated Corners," June 1, 1909, page 14, sec. 45.)

Closing Corners of section lines are to be restored in the same manner.

Note – When a Closing Corner on a Parallel is lost and the measurement of the section line indicates that it may have been established either north or south of the Parallel or boundary line, the surveyor is to assume that it was placed *on* the *straight line*, and must be *restored thereon* regardless of the distance from the ¼ sec. cor. on the section line to the Closing Corner, and in alignment with the Closing Corner found and the said ¼ sec. cor.

If the Closing Corner is on an East or West Boundary Line, the same rule governs.

To Restore the ¼ Section Corner on the Township Line Between Sections 6 and 31

Example 4. Required to restore the ¼ sec. cor. on the Township line between sections 6 and 31.

The field note length of the line is 78.50 chains. By the county surveyor's measurement it is 80.30 chains:

then,

78.50 : 80.30 : : 40.00 = 40.92 chains, the true length of the east half mile. And 80.30 − 40.92 = 39.38 chains, the true length of the west half mile.

Meander Lines

Leading judicial decisions hold that Meander Corners denote the point on the line between adjoining sections and land owners, without usually being the terminal corner of the land; and that meander lines are not strictly boundary lines, and no not confine the ownership to the exact area appearing on the official plats, but such ownership extends to the water which by the plat bounds the land and in the case of unnavigable rivers to the *aqua filium* or thread of the stream.

Where the United States has disposed of the fractional lots along the shores of meandered lakes and rivers, it does not claim any land which may have been left between the meander line and the water.

THE SUBDIVISION OF SECTIONS

1. SUBDIVISION OF SECTIONS INTO QUARTER SECTIONS

(a)   An Act of Congress approved February 11, 1805, established the method of subdividing sections into quarter sections, by running straight lines from the ¼ sec. cors. to the opposite corresponding corners and at the intersection of these lines shall be the *legal* center of the section and the common corner to the four quarter sections.

This law has never been repealed.

There is no exception to the rule.

(b)   That in fractional sections where no opposite corresponding ¼ sec. cor. has been or can be fixed, then the quarter lines shall be run from the established corners due north, south, east or west as the case may be, to the water course, Indian Boundary line or other external boundary of such fractional Township.   This is interpreted by the General Land Office to be a mean line between the opposite sides of the section actually run and marked.

2. SUBDIVISION OF QUARTER SECTIONS, INTO QUARTERS OR SIXTEENTHS

Preliminary to subdividing quarter sections of an interior section, 1-16 cors. will be established equidistant and on line between the section and ¼ sec. cors. and between the center of the section and the ¼ sec. cors. Then run straight lines between the opposite corresponding 1-16 cors. The intersection of these straight lines will be the *legal* center of the quarter section, and the common corner to the four quarter-quarter sections or sixteenths. Fig 3.

3. SUBDIVISION OF FRACTIONAL QUARTER SECTIONS IN THE NORTH AND WEST TIER OF SECTIONS OF THE TOWNSHIP

In the original survey of the section, the ¼ sec. cor. was established 40.00 chains from the last interior section corner, and the excess or deficiency of measurement was thrown into the last half mile.

By law this excess or deficiency is thrown into the last tier of forties and numbered as lots. The Government surveyor did not establish a 1-16 cor. at 20.00 chains from the ¼ sec. cor., or 60.00 chains from the section corner.

The following figure will illustrate the method of subdividing sections.

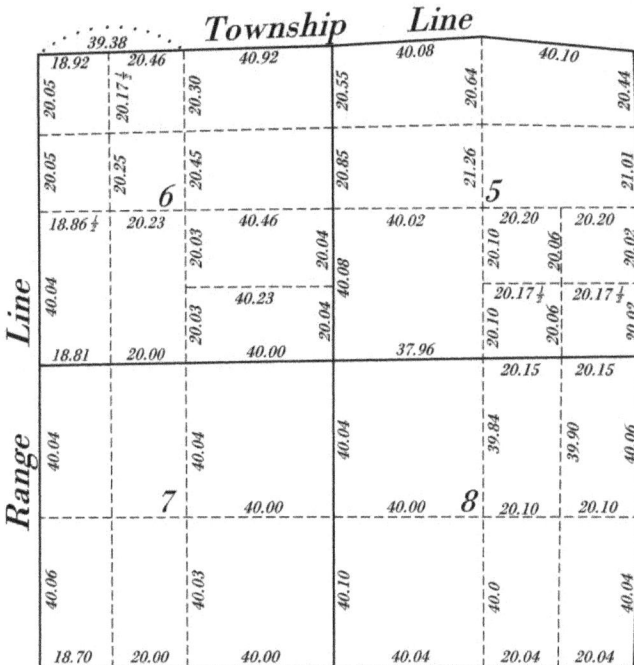

Fig. 3

Example 5. Required to establish the 1-16 cors. of fractional north or west half sections . . . . . Fig. 3.

Method. The government field note length of the north half mile between secs. 4 and 5, is 39.50 chains. By the county surveyor's measurement it is 41.50 chains, then,

(a) 39.50 : 41.50 : : 20.00 = 21.01 = the true distance from the ¼ sec. cor. to the *legal* point of establishing the 1-16 cor.; and 41.50 – 21.01 = 20.49 chains, the true distance from the 1-16 cor. to the sec. cor.

The field note length of the north half mile between secs. 5 and 6, is 39.70 chains. By the county surveyor's measurement it is 41.40 chains. Then,

(b) 39.70 : 41.40 : : 20.00 = 20.85 chains=the true distance from the ¼ sec. cor. to the *legal* point of establishing the 1-16 cor.; and 41.40 – 20.85=20.55 chains, the true distance from the 1-16 cor. to the sec. cor.

It is now required to find the *legal* point of location for the 1-16 corner between the center of the section and the ¼ sec. cor. on the township line.

(c) 39.50, in (a) + 39.30 in (b) = 78.80 ÷ 2 = 39.40 chains, the true mean or Government distance from the center of the section to the ¼ sec. cor.

By the county surveyor's measurement this distance is 41.90 chains. then,

(d) 39.40 : 41.90 : : 20.00=21.26, the true distance from the center of the section to the 1-16 sec. cor.; and,

41.90–21.26=20.64 chains, the true distance from the 1-16 sec. cor. to the ¼ sec. cor.

It will be observed that 41.90 in proportion (c) is not the mean of the county surveyor's measurement of the fractional half miles in (a) and (b); this is accounted for by reason of the ¼ sec. cor. on the township line not being on a straight line with the section corners, which has the effect of causing an angle or crook in the line running east and west, which very often occurs and cannot now be corrected. If the county surveyor had previously ascertained that the ¼ sec. cor. was on a straight line with the section corners, then the mean of his distance would be the second term in proportion (d).

All the other fractional sections of the township are subdivided in the same manner, *except* section 6.

SUBDIVISION OF SECTION 6

Section 6 is subdivided in a manner similar to the other fractional sections, excepting the northwest quarter section.

The west half mile of the north boundary of sec. 6 (if a Township line) being fractional, the 1-16 sec. cor. is established at proportional distances between the ¼ sec. cor. and the Township Corner; but on the north half mile of the west line of the section, it is established equidistant between the ¼ sec. cor. and the Township Corner. On the north and south, east and west quarter line, the 1-16 sec. cors. are established according to the principals explained in Example 5.

Straight lines are then run between the opposite 1-16 sec. cors. and at their intersection, is the *legal* center of the northwest quarter of section 6.

If the north boundary of section 6 is a Standard Parallel or Boundary line, the west line of section 6 is generally fractional, in such cases the 1-16 sec. cor. on the north half mile must be located *proportionally,* and *not equidistant.*

LINES CLOSING ON STANDARD PARALLELS AND BOUNDARY LINES

How to proceed when closing corners of lines, closing on Standard Parallels, Indian Reservations or Boundary Lines, are not found on Straight lines connecting the nearest corners.

When closing corners of lines closing on Standard Parallels, Indian Reservations or Boundary lines, are not found on said lines but at a distance from it, the surveyor, subdividing the fractional section should preserve the Parallel or Boundary line as a *straight line*, and not regard the corner found as the proper corner of the fractional section, but it is to be considered as only fixing the position or direction of the line between the two fractional sections. He should therefore establish a corner on line with the corners of the fractional section at its *intersection* with the Parallel or Boundary line. He should *not destroy* the original closing corner, but preserve it as a witness by noting the distance and bearing to the new corner.

The ¼ sec. cors. of Fractional Sections on Parallels and Boundary Lines.

(a) The government did not establish ¼ sec. cors. on that side of sections rendered fractional by closing on Standard Parallels or Boundary lines, and it devolves on the county surveyor to establish the same equidistant between the Closing Corners of the section and on line with the nearest corners of the Parallel or Boundary line.

(b) In such fractional sections, as sec. 6, the ¼ sec. cor. is to be established proportionately.

If the sectional closing corners are found *off* the line, then the ¼ sec. cor. is to be placed on the Parallel or Bound-

58

ary line, equidistant between the new closing corners explained in (a).

The surveyor cannot fail to have observed in the discussion of the subdivision of fractional sections that the 1-16 cors. separating the fractional parts are established by proportionate measurement. He must bear in mind that the distance given in the Government field notes is the *absolute length*, and is the *standard of measurement* for that particular line, and any difference between that and his measurement is *not* to be considered as belonging to the fractional part, but proportionately to every chain and link of the entire distance.

It is illegal to restore the ¼ sec. cor. by simply measuring 40.00 chains from the section corner. It should be placed on line and equidistant between the section corner and ¼ sec. cor. except in the fractional miles when they should be proportionally.

It is illegal to establish the 1-16 cor. by only measuring 20.00 chains from the section corner, or ¼ sec. cor.; it should be placed on line and equidistant between the corners, except in the fractional part of the section when it should be proportionally.

It is illegal to establish the 1-16 cor. at 20.00 chains from the ¼ sec. cor. in the fractional half sections, thereby throwing all the excess or deficiency into the fractional part; it should be proportionally.

To the surveyor who has fallen into the error of establishing the 1-16 corners at 20.00 chains by *his* measurement from the ¼ sec. cor., thereby throwing all the excess or deficiency into the fractional part, we emphasize the remark that it is *wrong*, unjust to the adjacent land owners and *wholly* illegal. *It must be established proportionally.*

Note. A common practice of some surveyors in sub-dividing sections into quarter sections, is to run from one of the ¼ section corners 40.00 chains and establish the center of the section; and to run from the 1-16 sec. cor. 20.00 chains and establish the center of the quarter section; this practice being wholly illegal, binds no one to conform to it; and the surveyor who records such a survey subjects himself to the severest criticism in the future.

"The practice of entering a section to survey a tract from only one or two corners, and those perhaps unreliable, is unwarranted, and may result in litigation." General Land Office Circular, June 1, 1909.

PERPETUATION OF CORNERS

Government monuments being the basis of our surveys, should as speedily as possible be perpetuated in the most permanent manner with indestructible material.

Corners used as initial or closing points in a survey which have not been properly perpetuated and recorded in the Official Record of the county, should be thoroughly examined to satisfy the surveyor as to their identity.

If a stone, remains of the decayed post, charcoal or other memorial, clearly indicating the position of the corner, is found, it should be perpetuated at that point, or if witness trees are found, then, where the bearings and distances indicate it to have been.

The trench and witness pits were presumed to be at uniform distances from the corner unless otherwise stated in the record; but the evidence of their actual location as found by surveyors indicate that the distances were not always measured, but often estimated, and that the opposite pits were *generally* dug on line with the corner. Therefore, when four pits are found and no evidence of the corner itself exists, then the corner should be established at the *intersection* of straight lines between the center of opposite pits.

When only two pits are found such as the N. and E. or N.E. and N.W. pits, in the absence of indication of the corner, it is impossible to determine (from appearances of the ground) whether in the former case they were N. and E. or S. and W. pits; or in the latter case if they were N. E. and N. W. or S. E. and S. W. pits; and it would be the same were they the N. E. and S. E. or N. W. and S. W. pits. The surveyor must depend, in such cases, on which side the measurement and alignment falls between known corners, and his good judgment as to where the corner is to be finally established.

At ¼ sec. cors. where only two pits were dug, and they are in the direction of the section line, the corner, in the absence of other evidence, is to be established equidistant and on line between the center of the opposite pits; and where the pits were dug across the line, one in each section, the corner is to be established in the same manner, *unless* a straight line between the section corners should place it a little nearer one pit than the other; then the *presumption* is that it was originally on a straight line and it will be better to so establish it.

Witness pits should never be "dug out" or destroyed, but preserved as far as possible for the outline of the pits and the deposit which nature has placed therein serve as witnesses and take the place of witness trees in the prairie country, and it is unlawful to destroy the identity of witness pits as it is to destroy witness trees; they may be witnessed by boring a hole in the center 2 or 3 inches in diam. x 18 inches or more in depth, owing to locality, and fill the cavity with slacked lime; then measure from this point to the corner and enter all the particulars in the field book.

All corners should be perpetuated with imperishable monuments; for this purpose a hole should be neatly dug at the exact point, 8 or 10 inches square by two or more feet deep owing to locality. In the bottom deposit a memorial of coal, cinders, earthenware, queensware, bottles or other enduring material; on top set a long stone, and let it extend just above the surface; around the stone deposit cinders, etc., or a different colored earth, or in lieu of stone drive a heavy gas pipe or shaft, three or more feet long (the longer the better); a hole bored in the earth with a post auger and the cavity filled with Portland Cement, brick set on end two and two, two or three feet deep, make an excellent corner. A hard pressed brick or paving brick with the description of the corner, date of month, day and year, with the surveyor's initials neatly cut with a sharp chisel, and placed deep in the ground at the foot or alongside of the stone or pipe, is an excellent memorial that will endure through all time.

The law enacted by the last Legislature makes it imperative that the county surveyor perpetuate all Government corners found in the course of his survey that are not well marked shall be perpetuated in a permanent manner and all corners he may establish or re-establish shall be by setting monuments of concrete, vitrified burned clay, iron or stone and deposit at the base thereof, at a suitable depth to protect it from loss or destruction a memorial of durable material upon which shall be inscribed the date and initials of the surveyor's name and where the corner is unquestionably a Government corner the letters G. C. (initials of Government Corner) shall be added. In marking the date, it will be sufficient to use the number of the calendar month, thus 5-15-13 would represent the date May 15, 1913.

Civil engineers, county surveyors, private surveyors, "locators" or any other person, under penalty of not less than $10 nor more than $50 for each offence, are forbidden to establish or perpetuate any corner in imitation of government corners either by digging "quadrangular trenches" and "witness pits," or "witness pits" in either dimension, distance or direction as adopted by the General Land Office at Washington, D. C. Revised Statutes, 1913, Sec. 8717.

This law should have been enacted many years ago, for the reason that corners made in imitation of Government corners after the lapse of many years, when the pits became filled, are taken by the local surveyors to be original corners, however erroneously they may have been placed. Surveyors without the experience gained by years of continual practice of searching for original corners are being constantly deceived in not being able to discriminate as to the difference in appearances and conditions of the original and imitated or false corners.

The state is, in general, sufficiently settled to warrant the doing away with witness pits and the adoption of a different method of witnessing corners. Every county surveyor should adopt such additional methods as are not provided by law.

The aim of the surveyor should be to perpetuate his corners with material different from other objects in the vicinity, and with material that will endure for ages.

Except in low wet land, wood soon decays in our soil, and should be avoided; besides, any person can drive a stake which in time may resemble the true corner driven about the same time.

If stone is used, they should be long enough to extend deep into the ground to defy the plow or road grader.

If a hole is dug to receive the corner and memorials, and it is made square, neat and clean its entire depth, and the material deposited in it around the corner is different in color, in will be in *marked contrast* with work done by other people.

When witness trees are taken, the bearings should be to the center, near the ground, and the distance carefully measured from the corner to the surface of the tree, and to this add half the diameter, or measure to the *center* on the side of the tree.

The surveyor should adopt a uniform method of perpetuating his corners.

He should be careful to record all the particular details of his work.

FIELD BOOKS

Most county surveyors use one field book from day to day until it is filled. Many counties now furnish their county surveyors with a separate field book for each township. When he goes into any particular township he takes the book for that township. Each book should be plainly marked on the cover with the number of township and range. The law provides that the county surveyor shall be provided by the county with field books, duplicates of the Official Record.

This office has in compliance with law, section 2, page 00, adopted a form of ruling for the page of field notes and of the map, duplicates of the Official Record which the surveyors will find simple and convenient, will prevent many errors and is in the interest of uniformity in recording notes among county surveyors.

The notes should be copied into the Official Record as soon as he reaches home, and not wait for a "rainy day."

Don't keep notes on scraps of paper, old letters, etc.; write them in your field book, and don't be afraid of recording too much.

GOVERNMENT FIELD NOTES

The County Clerk is the custodian of the certified Government field notes of his County, by law. It is *not* convenient or *safe* for the surveyor to take these into the field, and it is often very tedious to make copies when needed. It is much better for the surveyor before going into any particular township to copy the field notes of the entire township, in abbreviated form, into a small book; soon he will have the notes of every township in separate books, convenient in form and easily carried in his pocket for ready use.

THE OFFICIAL RECORD

The Official Record is the all important record of surveys kept by the county surveyor; in it should be recorded, in indestructible black ink, a true, concise and complete copy of the pencil notes taken in the field. The law provides that the left hand page of the open book shall be reserved for field notes and the right hand page for the map and certificates, and in accordance with sec. 2, page 00; this office has adopted a form of ruling of the field note page and arrangement of the certificates. On application county surveyors will be furnished with the names of blank book manufacturers who are complying with the law.

The county surveyors will find this uniformity of arrangement of the field book and Official Record with our plan of sectional Index a great improvement on the heretofore promiscuous method of keeping records.

The surveyor should copy his surveys into the Official Record as soon as he reaches his office; it will then be an easy and pleasant task.

Copy the bearing and length of every line and when the variation is taken give the time of day; note all distances to creeks, ravines, tops of hills or divides, and other objects along the line that may assist in identifying the line or corners in the future. At any corner whenever possible, the angle included between any two lines should be read and recorded on the plat for convenient reference as a valuable additional check on the direction of the lines. Make the record full and complete, and don't be afraid of recording too much; some little particular if too often left out, that often proves to be very important.

Write in a clear plain hand – the record is for *others* to read – not you – *you know* what it is.

READING THE INSTRUMENT

The instrument is read from the North and South points only. An object situated in a northeasterly direction, the bearing is read thus: N. 56° 30' E...14.20 chs. dist. (not E. 33° 30' N.) or if southwesterly S. 43° 10' W. (not W. 46° 50' S.)

READING THE VERNIER

From correspondence in this office some surveyors who have variation verniers on their instruments have difficulty in "turning off" the variation correctly. If the surveyor wishes to "turn off" 12° 30' E. let him set the Vernier at Zero, then turn the instrument until the needle points to N. 12° 30' E. and clamp. Now with the tangent screw move the Vernier's Zero mark to the left until it arrives at 12° 30', the needle will then point to "0" or north in the needle box.

Verniers are usually double, having thirty equal spaces on each side of the Zero mark which correspond precisely to twenty-nine half degrees on the limb. They, thus read to single minutes and are read in the same direction the vernier is moved.

STANDARD CHAIN

Every surveyor should have a standard chain or steel tape line 66 feet long, by which he should very often *compare or test his measuring chain*, and any variation in its length should be promptly corrected. A No. 12 spring steel chain 66 feet long, and brazed throughout its length, is light, easily carried and very correct. The Government surveys in Nebraska were made with a 66 foot chain divided into 100 links; with it, comparisons with the original distances are quickly made, and in the computation of areas the calculations are made decimally and therefore shorter. If the 100 ft. chain or steel tape is used, reductions must be made to make comparisons with the original notes and in computation of areas the process is longer, more difficult and liable to error. The No. 12 spring steel chain or a 66 ft. steel tape line graduated in links is therefore recommended.

Horizontal Measurement. The length of all lines must be obtained by horizontal measurement, and care must be taken to keep the chain stretched to its utmost tension. In ascending or descending steep hills the horizontal measurement must be preserved by taking half its length, or twenty-five, ten or even five links, and the lower end should be held high enough to preserve a horizontal direction so as to obtain the correct length when a loaded tally pin or plumb is let fall.

THE CHANGE IN THE MAGNETIC MERIDIAN AND ITS EFFECT IN SURVEYING

The Public Surveys of Nebraska were begun about ten years after the invention of Burt's Improved Solar Compass, and the records show that nearly all of the Parallels, Meridians and Township lines were coursed with that instrument as well as the greater part of the subdivisional lines.

This wonderful instrument was so mechanically constructed that the *true meridian* could be quickly determined independently of the magnetic needle, which was also a part of the mechanism of every instrument, while the bearings of lines were read from the horizontal plate, yet were referred to the declination or variation of the needle, which was recorded as a necessary part of the Government field notes; so the surveyor before he begins retracing a line must determine the true bearing from the recorded variation calculated for difference of time.

The magnetic meridian or line of *No Variation* is now near Toledo, Ohio, and is slowly moving westward, from some yet unknown cause, and will probably continue for the next 150 years, when it will reach its western elongation, and then begin its retrograde motion eastward like the swinging of a huge clock pendulum. The annual westward movement of this magnetic meridian has been determined at Omaha to be 4', and at the western Boundary 3', or 3'.5 for central Nebraska, about Range 20 West.

Application. A line in Range 17 E. was run at a variation of 12° 20' E. July, 1856.

Required the variation, in July 1903 to retrace the same line = difference in time is 47 years = 47 x 4' = 3°08'

12°20' – 3°08' = 9°12' E. the required variation.

The Daily Change of The Magnetic Needle. This consists of a daily swing of the needle through an arc of about 11' in the summer months and 5' in the winter months; beginning about sunrise the north end slowly swings eastward reaching its extreme variation, or elongation about 8 o'clock a. m. then it retrogrades, reaching its morning position or *true* meridian about 10:30 a. m. and its extreme western elongation about 1:30 p.m.; then it sets out on its return to the position from which it started in the morning, where it arrives about sundown or dusk.

The Hourly Change. The unequal movements of the

needle during the different hours of the day being slowest early in the morning and late in the evening, when near the period of eastern and western elongations, and the most rapid about 9 a. m. and 3 p. m.

Application. A mile line is run at 8 o'clock a. m. when the needle is at the eastern elongation and reading 11° 45' E. July 1st. If the surveyor should attempt to retrace the same line at 1:30 p.m. at the same variation, the north end of the line will have a west departure of 26 links. To retrace the line he should have made the following reductions, to-wit: (5'.7 + 5'.6) (the hourly change) = 11'.3; 11° 45' – 11'.3 = 11° 33'.7 E. and run at that variation.

But the line run at 8 a. m. did not define a line *due north*, but 5'.6 or 13 links *east* of north; and the line at 1:30 p. m. 5'.6 or 13 links *west* of north; the true line is therefore half way between the two, and should have been run at 8 a. m., at 11° 45' – 5'.7 = 11° 39'.3 E., and at 1:30 p. m. retraced the line at a variation of 11° 33'.7 + 5.6' = 11°39'.3 E., the *true Magnetic Meridian.*

To assist the surveyor, who must depend on the magnetic variation to determine the bearing of his lines, as well as to enable all the surveyors to make the proper record of the variation for future use, we append the following table compiled from the Reports of Magnetic work by the U. S. Coast Survey.

TABLE I.

FOR REDUCING AN OBSERVED DECLINATION TO THE AVERAGE DECLINATION OF THE DAY

	Forenoon hours							Afternoon hours					
Mean local time	6 a.m.	7H	8H	9H	10H	11H	Noon	1H	2H	3H	4H	5H	6H
	E.	E.	E.	E.	E.	W.	W.	W.	W.	W.	W.	W.	W.
Dec., Jan., Feb. Northern stations.	0.7	1.1	1.9	2.2	1.5	0.1	1.8	2.9	2.8	2.1	1.3	0.7	0.2
March, April, May Northern stations.	2.6	3.8	4.4	3.5	1.2	1.6	3.8	4.8	4.6	3.8	2.5	1.4	0.7
June, July, Aug. Northern stations.	4.0	5.6	5.7	4.5	1.7	1.6	4.1	5.6	5.6	4.6	3.0	1.4	0.6
Sept., Oct., Nov. Northern stations.	1.8	2.6	3.1	2.5	1.0	1.5	3.3	4.0	3.4	2.3	1.2	0.6	0.1

             * East   *East

To exemplify the practical use of the above table, suppose at 4:00 p. m. April 15th the surveyor established a line and wishes to record the true magnetic declination of the needle. The north seeking end of the needle reads 11° 54' E.; add to this 2'.5 (the tabular W. hourly change) = 11° 56'.5, the true magnetic meridian. On the line April 16th at 9:00 a. m. the needle will read 12° 00' E.; to retrace the line subtract 3'.5 (the tabular E. hourly change) = 11° 56'.5 E., the true magnetic meridian, or the mean position of the needle between the extreme east elongation at 9:00 o'clock a. m. and its west elongation at 4 o'clock p. m. (when using the table discard fractional minutes and take the nearest whole minute.) The surveyor should therefore record the exact time of day when the needle was read, and should he fail at any time to make the necessary reductions, the future surveyor will have all the requisite data to determine the true magnetic bearing of the line.

Surveyors, in the early surveys, relied upon the recorded variation as a basis of the permanent location of lost lines which was the source of a great deal of trouble and litigation. Too much stress has been placed on the reliability of the readings of the needle in the original surveys, owing to a lack of knowledge of the field practice of the surveyors; for it is known that much of the inaccuracies were caused by assuming a variation for whole townships and entire block of surveys.

It is therefore impossible to determine the amount of local magnetism for any particular locality by calculation.

The magnetic needle, owing to its daily and yearly changes, local attractions in the soil, proximity to wire fences, telephone lines, weather conditions, etc., should not be relied upon to give the direction of permanent lines, but may be used to advantage in running random or temporary lines in search for evidences of old corners.

The bearings of permanent lines should be determined by means of the Solar Compass or transit, observations on Polaris, daylight observations on the sun or by angles turned from lines, the directions of which have been previously ascertained. The direction of a line determined from an observation on Polaris is advised; from this the angles of the other lines of the survey can be obtained.

GENERAL REMARKS

The government surveyed the land while it owned it. The monuments on the ground mark the surveys; the land was disposed of according to the survey, and not according to the field notes.

A county surveyor has no authority whatever, to destroy or ignore a government corner; neither has a Road Supervisor, although it may be in his way when grading the roads; he should notify the county surveyor of its danger, so he can establish witnesses or find some way of perpetuating it. He should record his method.

Lines run to *divide sections* into their legal subdivisions, if erroneous *may be corrected*, for they are *subdivided by law*. If a surveyor makes a mistake, in running the subdivisional lines, it *can be corrected by running the lines according to law*.

In searching for corners careful manipulation is necessary; it may be easily destroyed by an ignorant and careless person striking deep into the ground with his spade.

The surveyor who unnecessarily drives wooden stakes for corners, discredits his own work, and is discredited in the minds of thoughtful landowners, who see future expense of again calling a surveyor to hunt up the rotten stake; they see disputes and perhaps future lawsuits.

All corners established by the government in a system of surveys have equal weight; thus ¼ sec. cor. has equal weight in determining boundaries as a section corner.

When the true line can be ascertained and parties by mistake agree upon an erroneous line, believing it to be the true line, they will not be concluded by such agreement from claiming to the true line when discovered, unless the statute of limitation has run, or equitable reasons exist for establishing the erroneous line; but if the true line cannot be ascertained with certainty, then an agreement establishing a line of division will be sustained. 13 Neb. 415.

The agreement should be recorded in the office of the County Clerk or Register of Deeds, and in the Official Record of surveys. Any interested land owner not joining in the agreement is not bound by it.

The county surveyor is not only the professional expert in determining the boundary lines between adjacent owners, but is very often by tacit consent the judge and jury in determining their rights, the arbiter in settling the differences between them; he should therefore be fair, honest and just; knowing no friend so good he would favor, to the injury of his neighbor; no person so great an enemy, he would wrong in the performance of his professional duties; make no statements or explanations he does not know or believe to be true. He can be one of the most useful members of society by justly and equitably deciding land disputes among neighbors, or he can stir up strife and cause lasting enmity by being unjust, partial and *indiscreet*.

Every county surveyor should establish a *true meridian*, he should frequently test his instrument, and keep an official copy of the magnetic readings of the needle.

In searching for original corners the county surveyor should have the benefit of all the known information. The recovery of the land-marks and monuments of the Government survey is the object sought for which all the valuable time and money is spent. The Government field notes are the records of the original surveys and every county should procure a certified copy for the surveyor's use. He cannot *safely* do his work without them.

The original field notes, maps and official books and papers, pertaining to the United States surveys of Nebraska are kept in a fire proof vault in the office of the Commissioner of Public Lands and Buildings, who by law is their legal custodian. County surveyors in their official capacity by law have personal access to them without charge.

Parties requesting information from this office will often save time and vexatious correspondence by giving the section, township and range and the exact nature of the controversy.

Applications for the services of the State Surveyor to settle disputes between land owners should clearly indicate on a map or otherwise all the known government corners in the vicinity so that the records in this office may be examined; all the material facts relating to the dispute should be given, *without* disclosing the names of the interested parties.

This office will at all times, endeavor to render to the surveyors of the state, all possible assistance it can, in the way of information, opinions or advice under the authority given by the law authorizing the issuance of this Circular of Instructions.

ROBERT HARVEY,

State Surveyor and Draughtsman

Approved March 16, 1914.

FRED BECKMANN

Commissioner of Public Lands and Buildings and Custodian of records of the Government surveys.

TABLE II

LATITUDE OF THE STANDARD PARALLELS

	40°	00'	00"
BASE LINE	40°	00'	00"
1st Standard Parallel	40	20	52
2d Standard Parallel	40	41	45
3d Standard Parallel	41	2	37
4th Standard Parallel	41	23	29
5th Standard Parallel	41	44	21
6th Standard Parallel	42	5	13
7th Standard Parallel	42	26	05
8th Standard Parallel	42	46	57
Nebraska – South Dakota Line	43	00	00

TABLE III

LENGTH OF A DEGREE OF LONGITUDE, IN CHAINS AND MILES, ON EACH STANDARD PARALLEL

	Chains	Miles
BASE LINE	4,244.47	53.059
1st Standard Parallel	4,222.86	52.787
2d Standard Parallel	4,201.07	52.513
3d Standard Parallel	4,179.15	52.239
4th Standard Parallel	4,157.09	51.962
5th Standard Parallel	4,134.81	51.685
6th Standard Parallel	4,112.46	51.406
7th Standard Parallel	4,089.92	51.124
8th Standard Parallel	4,067.22	50.840
Nebraska – South Dakota Line	4,052.96	50.660

TABLE IV

LATITUDE OF EACH MILE FROM THE BASE LINE TO THE NORTH BOUNDARY

Miles	40°	00'	00"	Miles	40°	25'	13"	Miles		49'	34"	Miles	41°	13'	55"
1			52"	29	40°	25'	13"	57	40°	49'	34"	85	41°	13'	55"
2		1'	44	30		26	05	58		50	26	86		14	47
3		2	37	31		26	58	59		51	19	87		15	39
4		3	29	32		27	50	60		52	11	88		16	32
5		4	21	33		28	42	61		53	03	89		17	24
6		5	13	34		29	34	62		53	55	90		18	16
7		6	05	35		30	26	63		53	47	91		19	08
8		6	57	36		31	18	64		55	39	92		20	00
9		7	50	37		32	11	65		56	32	93		20	52
10		8	42	38		33	03	66		57	24	94		21	45
11		9	34	39		33	55	67		58	16	95		22	37
12		10	26	40		34	47	68		59	08	96		23	29
13		11	18	41		35	39	69	41°	00	00	97		24	21
14		12	11	42		36	32	70			52	98		25	13
15		13	03	43		37	24	71		1	45	99		26	05
16		13	55	44		38	16	72		2	37	100		26	58
17		14	47	45		39	08	73		3	29	1		27	50
18		15	39	46		40	00	74		4	21	2		28	42
19		16	31	47		40	52	75		5	13	3		29	34
20		17	24	48		41	45	76		6	06	4		30	26
21		18	16	49		42	37	77		6	58	5		31	18
22		19	08	50		43	29	78		7	50	6		32	11
23		20	00	51		44	21	79		8	42	7		33	03
24		20	52	52		45	13	80		9	34	8		33	55
25		21	45	53		46	06	81		10	26	9		34	47
26		22	37	54		46	58	82		11	19	110		35	39
27		23	29	55		47	50	83		12	11	11		36	31
28		24	21	56		48	42	84		13	03	12		37	24

TABLE IV – Continued

LATITUDE OF EACH MILE FROM THE BASE LINE TO THE NORTH BOUNDARY

Miles	40°	00'	00"	BASE LINE											
Miles				Miles				Miles				Miles			
113	41°	38'	16'	141	42°	02'	36'	169	42°	26'	57"	197	42°	51'	17"
4		39	08	2		3	29	170		27	49	8		52	10
5		40	00	3		4	21	1		28	41	9		53	02
6		40	52	144		5	13	2		29	33	200		53	54
7		41	44	5		6	05	3		30	26	1		54	46
8		42	37	6		6	57	4		31	18	2		55	38
9		43	29	7		7	49	5		32	10	3		56	30
120		44	21	8		8	42	6		33	02	4		57	23
1		45	13	9		9	34	7		33	54	5		58	15
2		46	05	150		10	26	8		34	46	6		59	07
3		46	57	1		11	18	9		35	39	7	43°	00	00
4		47	50	2		12	10	180		36	31				
5		48	42	3		13	02	1		37	23				
6		49	34	4		13	55	2		38	15				
7		50	26	5		14	47	3		39	07				
8		51	18	6		15	39	4		39	59				
9		52	11	7		16	31	5		40	52				
130		53	03	8		17	23	6		41	44				
1		53	55	9		18	15	7		42	36				
2		54	47	160		19	07	8		43	28				
3		55	39	1		20	00	9		44	20				
4		56	31	2		20	52	190		45	12				
5		57	24	3		21	44	1		46	04				
6		58	16	4		22	36	2		46	57				
7		59	08	5		23	28	3		47	49				
8	42°	00	00	6		24	20	4		48	41				
9			52	7		25	13	5		49	33				
140		1	44	168		26	05	6		50	25				

INDEX

[End Original Pamphlet]

Biography

Robert Harvey was born on January 4, 1844, in Savannah, Ohio. Harvey's interest in surveying began at an early age. He developed a keen fascination with the land at the age of seven as he watched the county surveyor survey a neighbor's property. That attraction endured as his family moved to Noble County, Indiana. In August 1862, he enlisted in Company D, Seventy-fourth Regiment of the Indiana Volunteer Infantry and participated in the battle of Perryville. After being mustered out of service at Gallatin, Tennessee, he became a student at the surveying and engineering colleges at Adrian and Albion, Michigan. After graduation, while working for two county surveyors in Michigan, Harvey heard complaints about crooked lines and long and short half miles. Before he could address these issues, he still had much to learn about surveying the land.

Harvey married Emma H. Ames in 1868, and moved to Nebraska in 1869. Arriving in Omaha, he found employment on a government surveying crew. Harvey spoke with Surveyor General E. E. Cunningham in Plattsmouth regarding his desire to follow the surveying profession, explaining his need to gain knowledge of the standard methods used to perform government surveys. Harvey's schooling had taught him how the government surveys were made in the books, but he especially wanted to know how they were made on the ground. Cunningham gave Harvey advice on the operation of government crews, as well as the names of several deputies who would be receiving contracts that year in Nebraska. Harvey returned to Omaha and met U. S. Deputy Surveyor William J. Allason, who had been awarded contracts to establish standard parallels, guide meridians, township lines, section lines, and meander lines. The broadness of these contracts would immediately give Harvey experience in nearly every aspect of government surveying. Allason was impressed with Harvey's enthusiasm and willingness to work and hired him as a chainman on his crew. Harvey launched his surveying career in establishing the original government survey lines.

Harvey obtained a soldier's homestead in 1871 near St. Paul, Nebraska. There he became the Howard County deputy county surveyor and also the county surveyor in an area that had been surveyed by another government surveyor just four years earlier. In this location, Harvey befriended James N. Paul, a U. S. deputy surveyor and one of the two brothers for whom the town was named. The following year, Harvey was awarded his own government contracts to survey township lines and the interior subdivisions. He became a U. S. deputy surveyor in Nebraska just three years after arriving in the state. His dual roles, as the Howard County surveyor and as U. S. deputy surveyor in the summer, would consume his life for the next 30 years.

During a survey for the St. Paul cemetery in 1873, Harvey discovered several original government quarter section corners in the area just south of that city which were set by U. S. deputy surveyor Josiah B. Park, without having measured the lines across the entire section. This was perhaps Harvey's first personal discovery of a U. S. deputy surveyor short cutting his work. Due to his thoroughness, Harvey gained the favor of the surveyor general who was awarding the yearly contracts. During his many summers as a U. S. deputy surveyor, he endured extreme weather conditions, several confrontations with the Sioux Indians, and at least one narrow escape from a group of Apache Indians. During one skirmish with the Sioux, his survey party came under attack. Harvey's crew ultimately charged the camp and captured five teepees.

Harvey studied law in his spare time and was admitted to the bar in 1883, but he never pursued this career due to his desire to remain outside the confines of an office. His previous trials and accomplishments helped Harvey transition into the next chapter of his life.

Harvey's appointment as Nebraska's first state surveyor in 1903 at the age of 59 was a natural choice. No one knew the state better than him, and his memory went beyond that of the average man. As state surveyor, Harvey once again retraced the interior government section lines established by other U. S. deputy surveyors. While retracing these government surveys, Harvey took notice of the crooked lines and long and short half miles in Nebraska that he had heard surveyors complain about in other states for so long.

Often, there was no explanation for the government-established quarter section corners deviation from a straight line and an equal distance between the adjacent section corners. In the eyes of many surveyors, the vast, treeless, and often flat plains of Nebraska should have resulted in greater accuracy than those areas previously surveyed in the states to the east. Not all of the government surveys in Nebraska resulted in substandard work; in fact, most were accomplished according to the rules set forth in the instructions; however, there was sufficient evidence to suggest that many government surveys were not. As settlement grew westward, the once uninhabited regions of Nebraska, particularly the Sandhills region, began to acquire new homesteaders. In some remote areas, the government corners were probably not even established. Evidence suggests that the notes might have been fabricated since obvious topographical features were not mentioned. Many government survey crews were working in the same areas and friendships were formed among the various crews. If a pact had been made among the various crews to do substandard work, they figured it would be many years before it would be discovered.

All of these were logical reasons for the discrepancies, but the most obvious was that, in the early history of the state, many considered the Sandhills region in the northwest part of the state to be, for the most part, entirely worthless, or only adaptable for grazing purposes. Hundreds of townships were surveyed many years before a farmer or grazer had located there. Since the region was virtually void of timber or stone, the corners of the surveys were usually mounds of earth taken from the witness pits. By the time permanent settlement began, most had nearly been destroyed by wind and storm. Early deputy surveyors probably saw their work as merely a formality since they felt no one would actually ever attempt to live in that region.

Robert Harvey continued to serve as Nebraska's state surveyor until 1923. He became a member of the Nebraska State Historical Society in 1905, and served as its president from 1922-23. His contribution to the society was enormous since he had previously documented numerous historical sites during his many years of government surveying. Harvey undertook the project of locating the Oregon Trail through Nebraska before plows erased many of the ruts previously made by thousands of wagons. Most of Robert Harvey's surveying took place in Nebraska, except for his initial start in Michigan, some mining surveys in the Black Hills of South Dakota, and some brief government work in New Mexico. Harvey died at the age of 79 on November 1, 1923, and is buried in the St. Paul, Nebraska, cemetery.

Jerold F. Penry
2014

Robert Harvey
1844 – 1923

Nebraska State Surveyor
1903 - 1923